Presented to:

By:

Date:

Occasion:

Warner Books, Inc., 1271 Avenue of the Americas, New York, NY 10020

Visit our website at www.twbookmark.com

W WARNER*Faith* A Division of AOL Time Warner Book Group
The Warner Faith name and logo are registered trademarks of Warner Books, Inc.

Printed in the United States of America

First Printing: May 2003
10 9 8 7 6 5 4 3 2 1

ISBN: 0-446-53250-9
LCCN: 2003101815

THE POWER OF
DETERMINATION

Looking to Jesus

JOYCE MEYER

WARNER
Faith

CONTENTS

Part One:
I WILL NOT QUIT   9

His Way Is Not Too Hard   11
Determination   13
Hang Tough!   15
Keep on Keeping On   17
Set Your Mind and Keep It Set   19
Run the Race   21
Be Patient   23
Wait on the Lord   25

Part Two:
I WILL HAVE FAITH   29

Stop the Emotional Yo-yo   31
God Is Unchanging   33
God Is Always Good   35
The Lord Is Our Rock   37
A Rock-Solid Foundation   39
From Faith to Faith   41
At All Times   43
Keep on Walking   45

Part Three:
I WILL OVERCOME   49

Why Be Tested?   51
I Will Trust God   53
I Will Be Secure in Jesus   55
I Will Lean on God   57
I Will Shake Off Rejection   59
I Will Not Be Bitter   61
I Will Forgive   63
I Will Love   65

Part Four:
I WILL BE FAITHFUL   69

Faithful in Loneliness   71
Faithful in the Wilderness   73
Faithful to Obey   75
Faithful When Frustrated   77
Faithful When Discouraged   79
Faithful to Serve   81
Faithful When Misunderstood   83
Faithful to His Timing   85

Part Five:
I WILL STAY BALANCED   89

Restrict Yourself   91
Balance in Your Work   93
Balance in Your Finances   95
Balance in Your Diet   97
Balance in Everything   99
You Are Not Invincible   101
Get Some Rest   103
Determine to Prune   105

Part Six:
I WILL PRESS ON   109

Chosen by God   111
Be Usable   113
God Has a Plan   115
Go Against the Flow   117
Know What You're Doing   119
Refuse to Give Up   121
Do It Again!   123
Stay on the Narrow Path   125

I WILL
NOT QUIT

If you will obey God and never give in or give up, then nothing — no person on earth, no devil in hell, no inability you have, nothing from your past — will be able to keep you from being successful.

GOD'S WORD FOR YOU

*For this commandment which I command you this day
is not too difficult for you, nor is it far off.*

DEUTERONOMY 30:11

o n e

I WILL NOT QUIT

 o often, someone will come to me for advice and prayer, and when I tell them what the Word of God says, or what I think the Holy Spirit is saying, their response is, "I know that's right; God has been showing me the same thing. But, Joyce, it's just too hard." It is one of the most commonly expressed excuses I hear from people.

When I initially began to see from the Word of God how I was supposed to live and behave, and compared it to where I was, I also said, "I want to do things Your way, God, but it is so hard." God graciously showed me this is a lie the enemy tries to inject into our minds to get us to give up. God's commandments are not too difficult or too far away.

Walking in obedience to God is not too difficult because He has given His Spirit to work in us powerfully and to help us in all He has asked of us (John 14:16). He is in us and with us all the time to enable us to do what we cannot do, and to do with ease what would be hard without Him!

Things get hard when we try to do them independently without leaning on and relying on God's grace.

GOD'S WORD FOR YOU

When Pharaoh let the people go, God led them not by way of the land of the Philistines, although that was nearer; for God said, Lest the people change their purpose when they see war and return to Egypt.

EXODUS 13:17

～

For no temptation (no trial regarded as enticing to sin, no matter how it comes or where it leads) has overtaken you and laid hold on you that is not common to man [that is, no temptation or trial has come to you that is beyond human resistance and that is not adjusted and adapted and belonging to human experience, and such as man can bear]. But God is faithful [to His Word and to His compassionate nature], and He [can be trusted] not to let you be tempted and tried and assayed beyond your ability and strength of resistance and power to endure, but with the temptation He will [always] also provide the way out (the means of escape to a landing place), that you may be capable and strong and powerful to bear up under it patiently.

1 CORINTHIANS 10:13

～

His WAY IS NOT TOO HARD

God led the Children of Israel on a longer, harder route in the wilderness because He knew they were not ready for the battles they would face in possessing the Promised Land. He needed to do a work in their lives first, teaching them Who He was and that they could not depend on themselves.

You can be assured that anywhere God leads you, He is able to keep you. He never allows more to come on us than we can bear. We do not have to live in a constant struggle if we learn to lean on Him continually for the strength we need.

If you know God has asked you to do something, don't back down because it gets hard. When things get hard, spend more time with Him, lean more on Him, and receive more grace from Him (Hebrews 4:16). Grace is the power of God coming to you at no cost, to do through you what you cannot do by yourself.

God knows that the easy way is not always the best way for us. That's why it is so important that we not lose heart, grow weary, and faint.

Satan knows that if he can defeat us in our mind, he can defeat us in our experience.

GOD'S WORD FOR YOU

But Jesus looked at them and said, With men this is impossible, but all things are possible with God.

MATTHEW 19:26

DETERMINATION

Many people I meet want to start at point A in their Christian life, blink their eyes twice, and be at point Z. Many of them are frustrated about not knowing what their gifts are or what God has called them to do with their life. Some of them are so afraid of failing and making mistakes that it keeps them from stepping out.

We all have undeveloped potential, but we will never see it manifested until we believe that we can do whatever God says we can do in His Word. Unless we step out in faith, believing that with God nothing is impossible, He cannot do the work in us that He wants to do to develop our potential. It takes our cooperation and willingness through determination, obedience, and hard work to develop what He has put in us.

Nobody can be determined for us. We must be determined. If we are not determined, the devil will steal from us everything we have. So give your potential some form by doing something with it. You will never find what you are capable of doing if you never try anything. Don't stay in the safety zone. Step out into what you feel God is leading you to do, and you will soon discover what you really can do.

Most of us have no problem with wishbone;
it's backbone that we are lacking.

GOD'S WORD FOR YOU

And let us not lose heart and grow weary and faint in acting nobly and doing right, for in due time and at the appointed season we shall reap, if we do not loosen and relax our courage and faint.

GALATIANS 6:9

Hang Tough!

Losing heart and fainting refer to giving up in the mind. The Holy Spirit tells us not to give up in our mind, because if we hold on, we will eventually reap.

Think about Jesus. Immediately after being baptized and filled with the Holy Spirit, He was led into the wilderness to be tested and tried by the devil. He did not complain and become discouraged and depressed. He did not think or speak negatively. He did not become confused trying to figure out why this had to happen! He went through each test victoriously (Luke 4:1–13).

Can you imagine Jesus traveling around the country, talking with His disciples about how hard everything was? Can you picture Him discussing how difficult the Cross was going to be . . . or how He dreaded the things ahead . . . or how frustrating it was to have no roof over His head, no bed to sleep in at night?

Jesus drew strength from His heavenly Father and came out in victory. We have His Spirit dwelling inside us and the strength available to make it through whatever we are facing.

You and I have the mind of Christ, and we can handle life situations the way He did—by being mentally prepared through "victory thinking" rather than "give up thinking."

GOD'S WORD FOR YOU

So, since Christ suffered in the flesh for us, for you,
arm yourselves with the same thought and purpose
[patiently to suffer rather than fail to please God]. For
whoever has suffered in the flesh [having the mind of
Christ] is done with [intentional] sin [has stopped pleasing
himself and the world, and pleases God],

So that he can no longer spend the rest of his natural
life living by [his] human appetites and desires, but [he
lives] for what God wills.

1 PETER 4:1–2

KEEP ON KEEPING ON

Peter's beautiful passage teaches us a secret concerning how to make it through difficult times and situations. Here is my rendition of these verses:

"Think about everything Jesus went through and how He endured suffering in His flesh, and it will help you make it through your difficulties. Arm yourselves for battle; prepare yourselves for it by thinking as Jesus did . . . 'I will patiently suffer rather than fail to please God.' For if you suffer, having the mind of Christ toward it, you will no longer be living just to please yourself, doing whatever is easy and running from all that is hard. But you will be able to live for what God wills and not by your feelings and carnal thoughts."

There is suffering "in the flesh" that we will have to endure in order to do God's will. Trials and tests will come to develop the potential God has put in you. Your part is to determine that you are not going to quit, no matter what, until you see manifested what God has placed within you. There is one kind of person the devil can never defeat—one who is not a quitter!

Keep on keeping on, and you'll get there.

GOD'S WORD FOR YOU

And set your minds and keep them set on what is above
(the higher things), not on the things that are on the earth.

COLOSSIANS 3:2

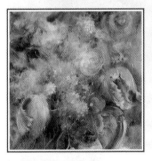

Set Your Mind and Keep It Set

We can have right and wrong mind-sets. The right ones benefit us, and the wrong ones hurt us and hinder our progress. We need our minds set in the right direction.

Some people see life negatively because they have experienced unhappy circumstances all their lives and can't imagine anything getting any better. Then there are some people who see everything as negative simply because their personality leans in that direction. Some people live in a wilderness of negativity, while others are a wilderness. Whatever its cause, a negative outlook leaves a person miserable and unlikely to grow spiritually.

With God's help and your hard work and determination, you can break negative mind-sets and old habits that are hurting and hindering you. The devil doesn't want you to break through because he knows that if you do, you will become a world changer. Your life will change, which will cause many other lives to change. If you develop your potential, it is going to have a positive effect not only on your life, but on someone else's life.

Your potential is a priceless treasure, like gold. All of us have gold hidden within, but we must be determined to dig to get it out.

GOD'S WORD FOR YOU

Wherefore seeing we also are compassed about with so great a cloud of witnesses, let us lay aside every weight, and the sin which doth so easily beset us, and let us run with patience the race that is set before us . . .

HEBREWS 12:1 KJV

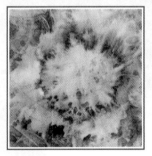

$\mathscr{R}$UN THE RACE

If we are going to run our race, we must lay aside every weight and sin and run the race with patience. In the days this verse was written, runners conditioned their bodies for a race just as we do today. But at the time of the race, they stripped off their extra clothing so that when they ran there would be nothing to hinder them. They also oiled their bodies with fine oils.

In our Christian life we need to remove anything that hinders us from running the race that God has set before us. We need to be well oiled or anointed with the Holy Spirit if we are going to win our race.

The devil has a thousand ways to entangle us and prevent us from doing what we are supposed to be doing. The world we live in is filled with constant distractions. Too many commitments, letting other people control our time, not knowing how to say no, or getting overly involved in someone else's problems instead of keeping our eyes on our own goals will keep us from fulfilling our potential.

We have to be determined that nothing
is going to hinder us from fulfilling God's plan
and purpose for our life.

GOD'S WORD FOR YOU

Consider it wholly joyful, my brethren, whenever you are enveloped in or encounter trials of any sort or fall into various temptations.

Be assured and understand that the trial and proving of your faith bring out endurance and steadfastness and patience.

But let endurance and steadfastness and patience have full play and do a thorough work, so that you may be [people] perfectly and fully developed [with no defects], lacking in nothing.

JAMES 1:2–4

BE PATIENT

James teaches us that we should rejoice when we find ourselves involved in difficult situations, knowing that God is trying our faith to bring out patience. I have found that trials did eventually bring out patience in me, but first they brought a lot of other junk to the surface—such as pride, anger, rebellion, self-pity, complaining, and many other things. It seems that these ungodly traits need to be faced and dealt with before patience can come forth.

The Bible talks about purification, sanctification, sacrifice, and suffering. These are not popular words; nevertheless, if I am to become Christlike in my character, I must go through such things and learn His ways. God's desire is to make us perfect, lacking in nothing. The devil cannot control a patient person.

I struggled with the process of change for a long time, but I finally realized that God was not going to do things my way. There were people and situations He placed in my life that made me want to give up and quit. But He did not want an argument from me. He only wanted to hear, "Yes, Lord. Your will be done."

Going through difficulties instead of attempting to avoid them will save you a lot of agony.

GOD'S WORD FOR YOU

For you have need of steadfast patience and endurance, so that you may perform and fully accomplish the will of God, and thus receive and carry away [and enjoy to the full] what is promised.

HEBREWS 10:36

Therefore humble yourselves [demote, lower yourselves in your own estimation] under the mighty hand of God, that in due time He may exalt you . . .

1 PETER 5:6

WAIT ON THE LORD

There are multitudes of unhappy, unfulfilled Christians in the world simply because they are so busy trying to make something happen, instead of waiting patiently for God to bring things to pass in His own time and His own way. We are in a hurry, but God isn't.

Humility says, "God knows best, and He will not be late!" Pride says, "I'm ready now. I'll make things happen my own way." A humble man waits patiently; he actually has a "reverential fear" of moving in the strength of his own flesh. Patience is the ability to keep a good attitude while waiting. But a proud man tries one thing after another, all to no avail. Pride is at the root of impatience.

Patience is a fruit of the Holy Spirit that manifests itself in a calm, positive attitude despite our life circumstances. Don't think you can solve all your problems or overcome difficulties on your own. As we humble ourselves under God's mighty hand, we begin to die to our own way and our own timing and to become alive to God's will and way for us. Character development takes time and patience.

It is only through patience and endurance in faith that we receive the promises of God.

I WILL
HAVE FAITH

You and I need to make a decision that, come what may, we are going to keep pressing on, looking to Jesus, no matter what.

GOD'S WORD FOR YOU

I am calling up memories of your sincere and
unqualified faith (the leaning of your entire personality
on God in Christ in absolute trust and confidence in His
power, wisdom, and goodness), [a faith] that first lived
permanently in [the heart of] your grandmother Lois and
your mother Eunice and now, I am [fully] persuaded,
[dwells] in you also.

That is why I would remind you to stir up (rekindle
the embers of, fan the flame of, and keep burning) the
[gracious] gift of God, [the inner fire] that is in you by
means of the laying on of my hands [with those of the
elders at your ordination].

For God did not give us a spirit of timidity (of
cowardice, of craven and cringing and fawning fear), but
[He has given us a spirit] of power and of love and of calm
and well-balanced mind and discipline and self-control.

2 TIMOTHY 1:5–7

t w o

I WILL HAVE FAITH

 have a feeling that in these last days we will need to be reminded of Paul's words of encouragement to Timothy of being willing to sacrifice or to suffer to fulfill the call of God on our life. Everything we have to do is not going to feel good all the time.

Timothy was a young minister who simply felt like giving up. The fire that once burned within him was beginning to grow cold. The church in those days was experiencing a great deal of persecution, and Timothy had some fears. Perhaps he felt worn out and that everything was crashing down upon him. We all feel at times that we just can't keep going.

Paul was saying, "Timothy, you may feel like quitting, but I want to see some stability in you. Remember the power of the Holy Spirit that changed your life. He gives you a spirit of discipline and self-control."

If we have stability, we do what is right when it feels good and when it doesn't feel good—whether it's praying or giving or any other obedience God is asking of us. If we ever want to see a release of our potential, we must display stability.

I don't know about you, but I have made up my mind that I will put my faith in God and His Word, come what may.

GOD'S WORD FOR YOU

But the fruit of the [Holy] Spirit [the work which His presence within accomplishes] is love, joy (gladness), peace, patience (an even temper, forbearance), kindness, goodness (benevolence), faithfulness,

Gentleness (meekness, humility), self-control (self-restraint, continence). Against such things there is no law [that can bring a charge].

GALATIANS 5:22–23

Stop the Emotional Yo-yo

I remember the years when I was what I call a "yo-yo Christian." I was continually up and down. If my husband, Dave, did what I liked, I was happy. If he didn't do what I liked, I would get mad. I was led by my emotions rather than the Holy Spirit within.

More than any other single thing, believers tell me how they feel. "I feel nobody loves me." "I feel my spouse doesn't treat me right." "I feel that I'll never be happy." "I feel . . . I feel . . . I don't feel . . . ," and on and on it goes.

God wants us to grow up and realize that our emotions are never going to go away, so we must learn to manage them rather than letting them manage us. We have to exercise self-control and tell our flesh to get in line with what is right rather than what it wants. We need to tell ourselves that we are not going to be able to say everything we want to say, eat everything we want to eat, stay up as late as we want, or get up when we feel like it. By the power of the Spirit, He will help us stop living by our emotions, and teach us to be stable.

As Christians, instead of concentrating on how we feel, we need to focus on what we know to be truth from the Word of God.

GOD'S WORD FOR YOU

Jesus Christ (the Messiah) is [always] the same, yesterday, today, [yes] and forever (to the ages).

HEBREWS 13:8

GOD IS UNCHANGING

What is the main thing that we love so much about Jesus? There are many answers to that question, of course, such as the fact that He died for us on the cross so we wouldn't have to be punished for our sins; then He rose again on the third day. But in our daily relationship with Him, one of the things we appreciate the most about Him is the fact that we can count on His unchanging nature. He can change anything else that needs to be changed, but He Himself always remains the same.

That is the kind of person I want to be, and God wants me to be, but it will never happen if I cannot control my emotions. Being emotionally mature means making decisions based on the leading of the Holy Spirit, not on our feelings. But it doesn't come naturally.

Just knowing these things is not going to make our emotions go away. But we have a God Who is able to bring us into balance. It doesn't mean we become emotionless or dull. God gave us emotions so we could enjoy life. But it does mean we take control in the strength and power of the Holy Spirit.

God does not want us to change every time our circumstances change. He wants us to always be the same, just as He is.

GOD'S WORD FOR YOU

Every good gift and every perfect (free, large, full) gift is from above; it comes down from the Father of all [that gives] light, in [the shining of] Whom there can be no variation [rising or setting] or shadow cast by His turning [as in an eclipse].

JAMES 1:17

GOD IS ALWAYS GOOD

James tells us that God is good, period. He is not good sometimes; He is always good.

Isn't it wonderful to have a God Who is unvarying? With God there is no turning, no variation. We have seen that His Son, Jesus, never changes. In John 10:30, we are told that Jesus and God are one and the same. If Jesus never changes, God never changes. Whether in the form of the Father, His Son, Jesus, or the Holy Spirit, God is always the same.

If we are having a hard time, if we feel like giving up, God is still good. If something bad happens to us, God is still good. God is a good God, and He wants to do good things for us. He doesn't do good things for us because we are good and we deserve them; He does good things for us because He is good and He loves us.

The world still needs to learn that truth. So do some in the church. It's a revelation that can blow away doubt and fear and discouragement. It can turn darkness to light!

The key to happiness and fulfillment is not in changing our situation or circumstances, but in trusting God to be God in our life.

GOD'S WORD FOR YOU

*He is the Rock, His work is perfect, for all His ways
are law and justice. A God of faithfulness without breach
or deviation, just and right is He.*

DEUTERONOMY 32:4

❧

*For they are a nation void of counsel, and there is no
understanding in them.*

*O that they were wise and would see through this
[present triumph] to their ultimate fate!*

*How could one have chased a thousand, and two put
ten thousand to flight, except their Rock had sold them,
and the Lord had delivered them up?*

*For their rock is not like our Rock, even our enemies
themselves judge this.*

DEUTERONOMY 32:28–31

❧

THE LORD IS OUR ROCK

God always loves us unconditionally. He doesn't love us if we are good and then stop loving us if we are bad. He always loves us. He is always kind, always slow to anger, always full of grace and mercy, always ready to forgive.

God is a Rock, unchanging and undeviating. He is great and unfailing, faithful and just, perfect and right in all His doing. He will never leave us or forsake us.

What would happen in our lives and in the lives of those around us if we were like God? What would happen if we were always loving, always slow to anger, always filled with grace and mercy, always ready to forgive? What would happen if we, like our God, were always positive, peaceful, and generous? He is our Rock, but He is also our Example. We are to strive to be the way He is.

I know that anyone can change if I can because I had a bad case of instability. God does not expect us to become perfect overnight, but He wants to help us to become more and more like Him day by day.

God wants you to come into a place of stability.
You will never be able to enjoy life as you
were meant to until you become stable.

GOD'S WORD FOR YOU

Now when Jesus went into the region of Caesarea Philippi, He asked His disciples, Who do people say that the Son of Man is?

And they answered, Some say John the Baptist; others say Elijah; and others Jeremiah or one of the prophets.

He said to them, But who do you [yourselves] say that I am?

Simon Peter replied, You are the Christ, the Son of the living God.

Then Jesus answered him, Blessed (happy, fortunate, and to be envied) are you, Simon Bar-Jonah. For flesh and blood [men] have not revealed this to you, but My Father Who is in heaven.

And I tell you, you are Peter [Greek, Petros—a large piece of rock], and on this rock [Greek, petra—a huge rock like Gibraltar] I will build My church, and the gates of Hades (the powers of the infernal region) shall not overpower it [or be strong to its detriment or hold out against it].

MATTHEW 16:13–18

A Rock-Solid Foundation

When Peter said that Jesus was the Christ, the Son of the living God, that was a statement of faith. In making this statement, Peter was displaying faith.

I don't think Peter just casually or nonchalantly made that statement. I think he did it with a surety and a certainty that impressed Jesus because He immediately turned to Peter and told him that he was blessed. Then He went on to say that it was upon this rock-solid foundation of faith that He would build His church.

Jesus was saying to Peter, "If you maintain this faith, it will be a rocklike substance in your life upon which I will be able to build My kingdom in you. Your potential will be developed to the place that even the gates of hell will not be able to prevail against you."

There have been many times in my life when I have been discouraged and not known what to do, or felt that nothing was working and that everybody was against me. The word I have heard over and over again is, "Only believe."

This promise was not just for Peter alone.
Jesus is saying the same thing to you and me.
Only believe!

GOD'S WORD FOR YOU

For therein is the righteousness of God revealed from faith to faith: as it is written, The just shall live by faith.

ROMANS 1:17 KJV

FROM FAITH TO FAITH

It has long been a goal of mine to learn how to live from faith to faith. A number of years ago the Lord revealed to me, "Joyce, you go from faith to faith to doubt to unbelief, and then back to faith to doubt to unbelief."

The trouble with the church today is that we have too much mixture and not enough stability. That mixture is evident in our speech, as we see in James 3:10: "Out of the same mouth come forth blessing and cursing. These things, brethren, ought not to be so."

Perhaps you feel as I did—like a flat tire. We get all pumped up and roll along fine for a while, but then the next thing you know we are flat again. Too often we operate at zero power level. We keep mixing positives and negatives. Our positives are deleted by our negatives, and we end up right back at zero. I don't know about you, but I don't want to operate at zero power.

It's time to determine to stop the negatives—in our thoughts, our words, and our actions.

Doubt comes in the form of thoughts that oppose the Word of God. We must determine to know the Word, then we can recognize when the devil is lying to us.

GOD'S WORD FOR YOU

Trust in, lean on, rely on, and have confidence in Him at all times, you people; pour out your hearts before Him. God is a refuge for us (a fortress and a high tower). Selah [pause, and calmly think of that]!

PSALM 62:8

⚬⚬⚬

I will bless the Lord at all times; His praise shall continually be in my mouth.

PSALM 34:1

AT ALL TIMES

We are not to have faith and trust in God once in a while or from time to time, but at all times. We must learn to live from faith to faith, trusting the Lord when things are good, and when things are bad. It is easy to trust God when things are good, but when things are going bad and we decide to trust God, that is when we develop character.

The psalmist also tells us we should bless the Lord at all times. There are several other Scriptures that tell us things to do at all times—resist the devil at all times, believe God at all times, love others at all times—not just when it's convenient or it feels good.

There will never come a time when we will not find temptation lurking around us. As long as we live in the flesh, we will have desires that bring hurt and damage. It is only by disciplining our emotions, our moods, and our mouths that we become stable enough to remain peaceful, whatever our situation or circumstances, so that we are able to walk in the fruit of the Spirit—whether we feel like it or not.

Since you can choose your own thoughts, when doubt comes you should learn to recognize it for what it is, say, "No, thank you," and keep on believing!

But the boat was by this time out on the sea, many furlongs . . . , beaten and tossed by the waves, for the wind was against them.

And in the fourth watch [between 3:00—6:00 a.m.] of the night, Jesus came to them, walking on the sea.

And when the disciples saw Him walking on the sea, they were terrified and said, It is a ghost! . . .

But instantly He spoke to them, saying, Take courage! I AM! Stop being afraid!

And Peter answered Him, Lord, if it is You, command me to come to You on the water.

He said, Come! So Peter got out of the boat and walked on the water, and he came toward Jesus.

But when he perceived and felt the strong wind, he was frightened, and as he began to sink, he cried out, Lord, save me [from death]!

Instantly Jesus reached out His hand and caught and held him, saying to him, O you of little faith, why did you doubt?

And when they got into the boat, the wind ceased.

MATTHEW 14:24–32

44

KEEP ON WALKING

Peter stepped out at the command of Jesus to do something he had never done before. As a matter of fact, no one had ever done it except Jesus.

It required faith!

Then Peter made the mistake of spending too much time looking at the storm. He became frightened. Doubt and unbelief pressed in on him, and he began to sink. He cried out to Jesus to save him, and He did.

In Romans 4:18–21, Abraham did not waver in his faith when he considered his impossible situation. He was aware of it, but he didn't get preoccupied with it. You and I can be aware of our circumstances and yet, purposely, keep our mind on something that will build us up and edify our faith.

The devil brings storms into your life to intimidate you. We glorify God when we continue to do what we know is right even in adverse circumstances.

When the storms come in your life, dig in both heels, set your face like flint, and be determined in the Holy Spirit to stay out of the boat! Very often the storm ceases as soon as you quit and crawl back into a place of safety and security.

I WILL
OVERCOME

*Just because I don't understand
what is going on in my life does not mean
God does not have a purpose for it,
or just because I don't feel good about
something does not mean it is not going
to work out for the best.*

GOD'S WORD FOR YOU

*Oh, let the wickedness of the wicked come to an end,
but establish the [uncompromisingly] righteous [those upright
and in harmony with You]; for You, Who try the hearts
and emotions and thinking powers, are a righteous God.*

PSALM 7:9

*But, O Lord of hosts, Who judges rightly and justly,
Who tests the heart and the mind, let me see Your vengeance
on them, for to You I have revealed and committed my
cause [rolling it upon You].*

JEREMIAH 11:20

three

I WILL OVERCOME

ll of our life is filled with constant challenges and difficulties that test our resolve and determination and the quality of our character. It would be a great mistake to overlook the fact that it is God Who tests our hearts, our emotions, and our minds.

How do we test anything? We put pressure on it to see if it will do what it says it will do. Will it hold up under stress? Can it perform at the level its maker says it can? Is it genuine when measured against a true standard of quality? God does the same with us.

It is very sad to me how many people never make it past the trying point. They lack the power of determination to pass the test and spend their whole life going around and around the same proverbial mountains. But in God's school we don't flunk. We just keep taking the test over and over until we pass it.

James 1:2–4 says that tests bring out what is in us. It is in times of trial that we become best acquainted with ourselves and what we are capable of doing. Peter didn't think he would ever deny Jesus, but he caved in when tested. As difficult as it was, that test was the step that shaped Peter into the man of God he eventually became.

God is not impressed with what we say we will do; He is impressed with what we prove we will do under pressure.

GOD'S WORD FOR YOU

*[You should] be exceedingly glad on this account,
though now for a little while you may be distressed by
trials and suffer temptations,*

*So that [the genuineness] of your faith may be tested,
[your faith] which is infinitely more precious than the
perishable gold which is tested and purified by fire. [This
proving of your faith is intended] to redound to [your]
praise and glory and honor when Jesus Christ (the
Messiah, the Anointed One) is revealed.*

1 PETER 1:6–7

WHY BE TESTED?

There are many tests that come our way every day. For example, our boss tells us to do something we don't want to do. Or we're going to pull into a parking space and someone zooms in and takes it. Or someone speaks rudely to us when we've done them a favor.

In 1 Peter 4:12, Peter tells us not to be surprised or dismayed by the tests that we have to endure because by them God is testing our "quality," or our character. Peter knew the value of being tested in his own life. We all go through them, and we shouldn't be confused about why they come our way. God is testing our heart to see what manner of person we are.

Every time God gives us a test, we can tell how far we've come and how far we still have to go by how we react in that test. Attitudes of the heart that we didn't even know we had can come out when we are in tests and trials. So, Peter concludes in verse 13 that we should rejoice with triumph in our suffering so that Christ's glory may be revealed through us.

Testing times that God permits in our life are actually for our benefit, despite how we feel while we're going through them.

GOD'S WORD FOR YOU

But He knows the way that I take [He has concern for it, appreciates, and pays attention to it]. When He has tried me, I shall come forth as refined gold [pure and luminous].

JOB 23:10

I WILL TRUST GOD

One of the tests we can expect to encounter in our journey with God is the trust test. How many times do we say to God, "What is going on in my life? What are You doing? What is happening? I don't understand." Sometimes the things happening in us seem to be taking us in the exact opposite direction of what we feel God has revealed to us.

This is where many people give up and fail and go back to something that will be quicker and easier for them. If you are in a place right now where nothing in your life makes any sense, trust God anyway. One lesson I've learned through the years is this: There is no such thing as trusting God without unanswered questions. As long as God is training us to trust, there are always going to be things in our life we just don't understand.

When heaven is silent, I have learned that I need to stay busy doing the last thing God told me to do and just keep trusting Him. God will make all the pieces of our life work together for His purpose, even when we don't see tomorrow's provision. Tomorrow's answers usually don't come until tomorrow.

We must determine to trust God when we don't understand what is going on in our life.

GOD'S WORD FOR YOU

For we [Christians] are the true circumcision, who worship God in spirit and by the Spirit of God and exult and glory and pride ourselves in Jesus Christ, and put no confidence or dependence [on what we are] in the flesh and on outward privileges and physical advantages and external appearances . . .

PHILIPPIANS 3:3

I am the Vine; you are the branches. Whoever lives in Me and I in him bears much (abundant) fruit. However, apart from Me [cut off from vital union with Me] you can do nothing.

JOHN 15:5

$\mathscr{I}$ Will Be Secure in Jesus

God despises independence. He wants us to be as totally dependent and reliant upon Him as a branch is on a vine. We are not to put confidence in the flesh, not ours or anybody else's.

How many times have you trusted in your own strength and failed miserably? How many times have other people let you down after you put your trust in them? How many times have you been disappointed when others rejected you or failed to do what you expected? God will keep taking us through these tests until we put our confidence in Him alone. The tests don't change, but we change.

Some people spend their whole lives trying to make everybody and everything else change—trying to control other people, trying to control their circumstances—without realizing the real source of their misery and unhappiness. We are in for constant failure and disappointment as long as our security is in ourselves or other people. We will be held hostage to certain things to make us happy and never get around to changing because we expect everyone and everything else to change.

We must determine to allow the tests in our lives to cause the impurities in us to rise to the top where they can be dealt with.

GOD'S WORD FOR YOU

Cease to trust in [weak, frail, and dying] man, whose breath is in his nostrils [for so short a time]; in what sense can he be counted as having intrinsic worth?

For behold, the Lord, the Lord of hosts, is taking away from Jerusalem and from Judah the stay and the staff [every kind of prop], the whole stay of bread and the whole stay of water . . .

ISAIAH 2:22—3:1

I WILL LEAN ON GOD

God asks us through the prophet Isaiah, "Why are you putting your trust in weak, frail, and mortal people? In what sense can they be counted on as having intrinsic worth? Instead, put your trust in Me." In light of that, He adds that He is taking away from His people all their props.

What happens to us when our props are pulled out from under us? We discover what we are really leaning on, what we are really rooted and grounded in.

As new believers in Christ, when we begin our walk with God we need a prop system, something to help us on our way. We need a group of people around us to keep us studying the Bible, praying, and seeking the Lord. Without that support system, when the storms of life come against us, they will blow us over.

That support system may take many forms, but sooner or later God is going to start removing the props from under us. At first, this is pretty scary because we don't understand it or like it. It is then we discover how much of our sense of value and worth depends on the things we are doing. Our place is to cooperate with the Lord while He does His work in our lives.

We must put our roots down deep in Christ so that we can stand tall and steady and be a tree of righteousness.

GOD'S WORD FOR YOU

Remember that I told you, A servant is not greater than his master [is not superior to him]. If they persecuted Me, they will also persecute you; if they kept My word and obeyed My teachings, they will also keep and obey yours.

JOHN 15:20

He who hears and heeds you [disciples] hears and heeds Me; and he who slights and rejects you slights and rejects Me; and he who slights and rejects Me slights and rejects Him who sent Me.

LUKE 10:16

I WILL SHAKE OFF REJECTION

People will reject us just as they rejected Jesus, Paul, and the other apostles and disciples. We are servants of a rejected Master, and He leads us to do things that are different from what others around us are doing. But it is especially hard when we are rejected by people who are wrong and who are saying and doing wrong things.

When I first started preaching, I was terribly insecure and took my share of criticism and rejection. Finally, after struggling through embarrassments and feeling bad, the Lord simply said to me, "I am the One Who called you. Don't worry what people think. If you do, you are going to be worrying all your life because the devil will never stop finding people who will think something unkind about you."

In Acts 28:1–5, when Paul was bitten by a snake, the natives of the island of Malta thought he must be a murderer and their avenging goddess of justice would not allow him to live. Paul simply shook off the snake and suffered no evil effects. That is what we must do with fear, rejection, discouragement, disappointment, betrayal, or loneliness—shake it off and go on.

Even when our rejection is from people who are close to us, we must determine to keep pressing on toward fulfilling what God has called us to do.

GOD'S WORD FOR YOU

*But Jesus said to him, Judas! Would you betray and
deliver up the Son of Man with a kiss?*

LUKE 22:48

$\mathscr{I}$ WILL NOT BE BITTER

Jesus bore our sins so we do not have to bear them. But there are other things He went through that He endured as an example for us, things that we will have to follow in His footsteps and go through. Jesus faced the betrayal of Judas at the worst moment of His life but did not let it hinder Him. And it came in the form of a kiss.

Satan loves betrayal because often when we are hurt by someone we love, respect, and trust, we feel we can't trust anyone. Think of what David felt with Absolam, or Joseph with his brothers. We want to give up and "do our own thing" so we never have to experience that hurt again. Betrayal is something we must learn to shake off and not let hinder us, no matter how we feel.

In Matthew 24:10–13, Jesus warns us that in the last days betrayals will increase. He also tells us that those who endure to the end will be saved. As believers, it is not what happens to us that ruins us. It is our wrong response to what happens that ruins us. We can choose to make a right response.

❧

We must determine that with God's help we will allow our pain to make us better, not bitter.

GOD'S WORD FOR YOU

And the Lord turned the captivity of Job and restored his fortunes, when he prayed for his friends; also the Lord gave Job twice as much as he had before.

JOB 42:10

I WILL FORGIVE

One need not read far in the Bible to see the need of forgiving others. Many of the heroes of the Bible—Moses, Paul, Joseph, Stephen, Jesus, and others—had to forgive others for unthinkable hurts and wrongs.

But I will point out the case of Job, whom God told to pray for his friends who did not stand with him in his pain and suffering when he lost everything, but who judged him severely. Not only was their counsel unfair and cruel, but it was couched and twisted in spiritual words that must have pierced into Job's despair. As a result of his prayer and his forgiveness of them, Job received a double blessing from God.

The test of forgiveness comes in all sizes—from petty issues to cruelty and persecution. At whatever level, Satan knows that if we do not forgive, our faith will not work. Everything that comes from God comes by faith. And if our faith doesn't work, we are in serious trouble.

The heart of Jesus was never to return evil for evil, but to be charitable, unselfish, speaking kind words to those who harmed Him. That is His way for us.

We must determine to walk in the power of God's love and forgiveness, no matter what hatred, bitterness, or malice we may face.

GOD'S WORD FOR YOU

For if you love those who love you, what reward can you have? Do not even the tax collectors do that?

MATTHEW 5:46

I WILL LOVE

We all have a few people in our life who are like sandpaper to us. Some are like an entire package of sandpaper. It seems that when they are around, we are surrounded by sandpaper on all sides, grinding away on our rough edges.

When God first called me to preach, God put three people in my life who irritated the daylights out of me. One was my husband, Dave, who never seemed to do things the way I wanted them done. Another was a friend who was a perfectionist, who saw life in a way that drove my choleric personality crazy. The other was a girl who lived next door who was really vague about everything she wanted to do, while I felt I excelled in setting goals and being definite in everything I wanted to do. The sandpaper was grinding on me.

I thought everybody else had a problem. I resisted all the things I now know God had placed in my life. Then I discovered that God puts irritating people in our lives so we can't get away from them. If we try to run from one, two more will appear around the corner. We must learn to love and to get along with each other. Not everyone is going to be or do what we want.

We must determine to walk in the love of Christ and let Him shape us through others He brings into our lives.

65

I WILL
BE FAITHFUL

We must determine that we will be faithful, even when nobody knows us or seems to care what we are doing or going through. Never leave anything God has assigned you to do unless He Himself releases you from it.

GOD'S WORD FOR YOU

And let them also be tried and investigated and proved first; then, if they turn out to be above reproach, let them serve [as deacons].

1 TIMOTHY 3:10

four
I WILL BE FAITHFUL

e are all going to be tested. Count on it. There are no exceptions—everybody goes through different tests at times in their lives. But they are all open-book tests; the answers are found in the Book. No matter what we are going through, the Bible has the revelation that God has placed there for us.

We must be faithful to keep on doing what is right, even when the right thing has not happened to us yet. If we want God to work through our lives, He is going to do a work in us first. Satan attacks us in our minds, telling us lies such as, "This is not working. This is not doing you any good now, and it's never going to do you any good. You might as well give it up and go do something else." So many people quit on God right before their breakthrough.

Today's instant society is ruining people because we think everything should be easy. But godly strength, wisdom and knowledge, spiritual maturity and character are developed in us as we go through tests.

If we want to grow up in God and do what He has called us to do, we have to just settle down and be faithful. There is no "microwave maturity."

GOD'S WORD FOR YOU

Because he has set his love upon Me, therefore will I deliver him; I will set him on high, because he knows and understands My name [has a personal knowledge of My mercy, love, and kindness—trusts and relies on Me, knowing I will never forsake him, no, never].

He shall call upon Me, and I will answer him; I will be with him in trouble, I will deliver him and honor him.

With long life will I satisfy him and show him My salvation.

PSALM 91:14–16

FAITHFUL IN LONELINESS

God wants you to know that you are never alone. Satan wants you to believe you are all alone, but you are not. He wants you to believe that no one understands how you feel, but that is not true. In addition to God being with you, many believers know how you feel and understand what you are experiencing.

When you are making spiritual progress, Satan often brings affliction to discourage you and will try to make you feel alone. Several years ago I went through a very difficult time when I was separated from many people and things very dear to me. God wanted me to move on with my life, but I was not obeying Him. When I would not move, God moved me and some of the people in my life. I realize now that it was one of the best things that ever happened to me, but at the time I thought my whole world was falling apart.

Death, divorce, losing a career, or experiencing a personal injury are some of the devastating losses that people face. If you are battling loneliness and pain, draw strength from God and know that you are moving forward. He has the power to turn your mourning into joy and to comfort you in your sorrow.

*I will hope in God's love and believe
that God is always at my side.*

GOD'S WORD FOR YOU

*O God, You are my God, earnestly will I seek You;
my inner self thirsts for You, my flesh longs and is faint for
You, in a dry and weary land where no water is.*

PSALM 63:1

FAITHFUL IN THE WILDERNESS

One of the ways God tests us is by allowing us to go through dry times, times when nothing seems to minister to us or water our soul. We go to church, and we feel no different when we leave than we did when we came. Times when our prayers seem dry and the heavens are brass, times when we can't hear or feel anything from God.

I have gone through mountaintop times, and I have been through valley times. I have had dry times in my prayer life and in my praise and worship. There have been times when I could hear from God so clearly, and there have been other times when I have not heard anything at all.

I will be honest with you. I came to a point where I don't let how I feel determine whether I believe God is with me or not. I just choose to believe He is. I just love God, and that's it. I worship Him, and that's it. I pray, I believe He hears me, and that's it. I refuse to have the ups and downs I used to go through.

I will simply trust that God knows what He is doing. If I do or don't feel anything, that's fine. I will be faithful in the wilderness as well as on the mountaintop.

GOD'S WORD FOR YOU

How have you fallen from heaven, O light-bringer and daystar, son of the morning! How you have been cut down to the ground, you who weakened and laid low the nations [O blasphemous, satanic king of Babylon!]

And you said in your heart, I will ascend to heaven; I will exalt my throne above the stars of God; I will sit upon the mount of assembly in the uttermost north.

I will ascend above the heights of the clouds; I will make myself like the Most High.

ISAIAH 14:12–14

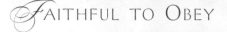 FAITHFUL TO OBEY

It was self-will that destroyed Lucifer. In exalting himself, he said, "I will," five times. God had an answer for him: " . . . you shall be brought down to Sheol (Hades), to the innermost recesses of the pit." In other words, "You will be cast down to hell."

When God asks us to do something contrary to our will, we must remember the words of Jesus: ". . . not what I will [not what I desire], but as You will and desire." This is perhaps the hardest test to pass and pass quickly. When we want something, we don't give up easily. It takes a lot of brokenness to bring us to the place where we are pliable and moldable in the hand of God.

The bottom line is that we must be willing to do whatever God says, and not what we feel or want. He may ask us to give away things we don't want to part with. He may ask us to go places, do things, and deal with people we don't want anything to do with. He may tell us to keep our mouths shut when we want to blast someone.

I will be faithful to always put God's will ahead of my own.

GOD'S WORD FOR YOU

I do not frustrate the grace of God: for if righteousness come by the law, then Christ is dead in vain.

GALATIANS 2:21 KJV

ℱAITHFUL WHEN FRUSTRATED

I know what frustration is like because I spent many years in frustration. I knew nothing of the grace of God. I have since learned that when I get frustrated, it is almost always because I am trying to make something happen instead of waiting on the Lord to make it happen. If I am frustrated, it is a sign that I am acting independently.

Are you frustrated with your spiritual growth? Does it seem the more you pray and seek God, the worse you get? Are you wrestling with an area of your personality that is causing you problems, or is there a specific bondage in your life that you can't break?

Frustration comes from trying to do something you cannot do. God is the only One Who can make things happen for you in your life. It will do no good to try to kick the doors down. But the minute you say, "Lord, I can't do this, so I let it go," you can almost feel the frustration lift off you by the grace of God.

I will let go and trust God
to do what only He can do.
I will let God be God.

And Saul said to David, You are not able to go to fight against this Philistine. You are only an adolescent, and he has been a warrior from his youth.

And David said to Saul, Your servant kept his father's sheep. And when there came a lion or again a bear and took a lamb out of the flock,

I went out after it and smote it and delivered the lamb out of its mouth; and when it arose against me, I caught it by its beard and smote it and killed it.

Your servant killed both the lion and the bear; and this uncircumcised Philistine shall be like one of them, for he has defied the armies of the living God!

David said, The Lord Who delivered me out of the paw of the lion and out of the paw of the bear, He will deliver me out of the hand of this Philistine. And Saul said to David, Go, and the Lord be with you!

1 SAMUEL 17:33–37

FAITHFUL WHEN DISCOURAGED

When David volunteered to go and fight Goliath, no one encouraged him. Everyone, including the king, told him he was too young, too inexperienced, too small, and he didn't have the right armor. But David encouraged himself by recounting the victories God had given him in the past.

Understand this: There will be hundreds, maybe thousands, of times when Satan will come against you to discourage you. He knows you must have courage to overcome the attacks he launches against you to keep you from being faithful to fulfill God's good plan for your life. If you are discouraged, you become weak and lose the courage to move forward.

When you have to wait a long time for something, or when it seems that everything and everybody is against you, you end up tired and worn out. Sometimes you are not ready to face the discouragement that accompanies it. Say to God, "Lord, I will be faithful to You. Help me now, or I will surely sink." Then get up and go on.

I will face my discouragement and refuse to have a pity party. I choose to be powerful in Christ rather than pitiful in myself.

GOD'S WORD FOR YOU

So when He had finished washing their feet and had put on His garments and had sat down again, He said to them, Do you understand what I have done to you?

You call Me the Teacher (Master) and the Lord, and you are right in doing so, for that is what I am.

If I then, your Lord and Teacher (Master), have washed your feet, you ought [it is your duty, you are under obligation, you owe it] to wash one another's feet.

For I have given you this as an example, so that you should do [in your turn] what I have done to you.

JOHN 13:12–15

FAITHFUL TO SERVE

God will give us opportunity to be a servant, and then He will check our attitude to see how we're doing. Jesus gave us an example of servanthood by washing the feet of the disciples and then telling them, "You should do to others as I have done to you."

Some people fail to be servants because they don't know who they are in Christ. They feel they must be doing something important, or they don't feel they are worth anything. They fail to see the value of doing whatever they are called upon to do, regardless of how ordinary or mundane it may seem.

We need to be willing to do whatever God wants us to do, to be used in whatever way He wants to use us. The attitude of a servant should be displayed in every area of our life. The servant test is simply how we respond to the opportunities God gives us to be a blessing to others. It reveals whether we really and truly want to be like Jesus. When God anoints a person, He is anointing that person to be a servant, not to be a famous person.

I will be faithful to wash some feet today, starting with those in my own home.

GOD'S WORD FOR YOU

No one understands [no one intelligently discerns or comprehends]; no one seeks out God.

ROMANS 3:11

FAITHFUL WHEN MISUNDERSTOOD

There are times when our faithfulness to God will be misunderstood by people we expect to understand and comfort us. I believe there will always be those who won't understand us. People did not understand Jesus either. Nobody really understood Him or the call on His life, not even His own family.

I remember when people would say to me, "Why do you act the way you do?" I have always been a little unique. What I mean by that is, I didn't always like what other people liked, or I didn't say or do things other people thought I should. I have always been really serious, and some people didn't understand me or my personality type.

Your obedience to God may mean that you won't fit into the regular regimen of what is going on around you. You may feel out of place, and in those moments it is really confusing and disturbing to be asked by other people, "What's wrong with you? Why do you act that way?" Remember that this is simply a test of your faithfulness.

I will stand with God and do what He says, even if nobody understands, agrees with, or supports me. Jesus understands me, and He is enough.

GOD'S WORD FOR YOU

But I trusted in, relied on, and was confident in You, O Lord; I said, You are my God.

My times are in Your hands; deliver me from the hands of my foes and those who pursue me and persecute me.

PSALM 31:14–15

❧

And lest I should be exalted above measure through the abundance of the revelations, there was given to me a thorn in the flesh, the messenger of Satan to buffet me, lest I should be exalted above measure.

For this thing I besought the Lord thrice, that it might depart from me.

And he said unto me, My grace is sufficient for thee: for my strength is made perfect in weakness. Most gladly therefore will I rather glory in my infirmities, that the power of Christ may rest upon me.

2 CORINTHIANS 12:7–9 KJV

❧

FAITHFUL TO HIS TIMING

God does not move in our timing. He is never late, but He is usually not early either. He is often the God of the midnight hour. It is as though we are a drowning man going down for the last time, and God comes through to rescue us at the last moment.

We must learn to trust God's timing. But before we can do that, we must come to the place where we are broken before Him. Our self-will and independence must be broken before God is free to work His will in our life and circumstances.

We see how this worked in Paul's situation. While God did not give Paul the breakthrough he wanted, He gave Paul the grace, strength, and ability to endure what he was going through and still walk in the fruit of the Spirit. One level of faith gets us delivered from trials, but another level of faith takes us through trials. Personally, I don't think it takes nearly as much faith to pray and get delivered from something as it does to continue to believe in God's power when deliverance is not being manifested. It is in those testing times that we grow in faith.

I will remain faithful and trust God to work in my situation—in His perfect timing. I will not take matters into my own hands.

I WILL STAY
BALANCED

*The source of many of our problems
is often not a big spiritual issue,
but a simple, practical area that demands
our full attention. We need to be balanced
in all of our life.*

GOD'S WORD FOR YOU

*Be well balanced (temperate, sober of mind), be vigilant
and cautious at all times; for that enemy of yours, the
devil, roams around like a lion roaring [in fierce hunger],
seeking someone to seize upon and devour.*

1 PETER 5:8

five

I WILL STAY BALANCED

 believe we live in a world that is out of balance. I also believe that most of the people in it are out of balance. Yet one of the things that we hear very little teaching about is the importance of being in balance.

The apostle Peter had several things to say on the subject. He tells us to be well-balanced and sober of mind, which means to be disciplined and serious. He also tells us to be vigilant and cautious because we have an enemy, Satan, who is out to seize upon and devour us.

In Ephesians 4:27, Paul emphasizes this same point when he tells us to control our anger, warning us, "Leave no [such] room or foothold for the devil [give no opportunity to him]."

If we are going to keep the door closed to the devil, we have to be determined to do so. He is looking for someone out of balance, someone who is paying too much attention to one area of his life and letting the other areas of his life go to pot, so to speak. We have to be determined to keep our priorities in line with God's priorities. Many times it comes down to simple, practical areas of our life that can mean the difference between keeping the door closed or not.

The devil is always going to give us trouble,
but we must do our part to keep the door closed to him.

Now every athlete who goes into training conducts himself temperately and restricts himself in all things. They do it to win a wreath that will soon wither, but we [do it to receive a crown of eternal blessedness] that cannot wither.

1 CORINTHIANS 9:25

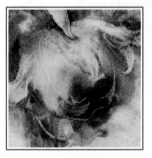

RESTRICT YOURSELF

First Corinthians 9:25 says that everyone who strives for mastery in anything must restrict himself in all things. This is all about the power of determination to keep our lives in balance.

Balance is not something we get into one time and stay there forever. We can be in balance on Monday and out of balance by Wednesday. It must be kept and maintained.

Nor is balance achieved over everything at once. There are thousands of areas of our life, and each one of them has to be brought into balance and then kept that way through regular maintenance and care.

We have a practical, natural side of our life that we must take care of. If we don't, it will end up hurting our spiritual side. For example, if we don't take care of our physical body, we will get sick. When we get sick, we don't feel like praying, releasing our faith, or believing the Lord. Satan looks for ways to get us out of balance so he can stop us from doing what God has called us to do.

When we have a problem, it is not always a spiritual area that is out of line. Many times it is a natural area that we are not paying attention to.

*By much slothfulness the building decayeth; and
through idleness of the hands the house droppeth through.*

ECCLESIASTES 10:18 KJV

BALANCE IN YOUR WORK

We have all been given powers and abilities. But we have to regulate the different areas of our life to keep them in proper perspective. If we have too much work and not enough rest, we get out of balance. We become workaholics and end up burned out.

I get a lot of satisfaction out of accomplishments and work. I don't like a lot of what I consider silliness and wasted time in my life. But because of my nature, I tend to get out of balance in this area. I have to determine that I will not only work but also rest. That is a priority for me.

But it is possible to go to the extreme and have too much rest and not enough work. Solomon says that "through indolence the rafters [of state affairs] decay and the roof sinks in, and through idleness of the hands the house leaks." In other words, people who don't work enough end up in trouble. Their houses, cars, bodies, and everything else become a mess because they don't do the work necessary to keep things in order. They fail to regulate the powers at their disposal. They are out of balance.

Bring order and balance to your life one step at a time. God is changing you day by day as you trust Him.

GOD'S WORD FOR YOU

Of what use is money in the hand of a [self-confident]
fool to buy skillful and godly Wisdom—when he has no
understanding or heart for it?

PROVERBS 17:16

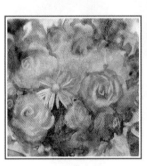

BALANCE IN YOUR FINANCES

We have the power to spend money or to save money. Some people try to save all their money. Either they are greedy or they are fearful about the future, thinking that money might save them from some unforeseen calamity. So they get out of balance.

Others get out of balance with money by over-spending all the time. When that happens, they start using credit cards and running them up to the maximum allowed. Some of them try to get out of debt by rebuking "the devils of debt." They want a miracle to correct their lack of discipline.

Too often that is our problem. We get ourselves into a mess and then try to get ourselves out by some miraculous method. We go from one mess to another, never wanting to take responsibility for our own mistakes. It is walking in stupidity to spend our lives ignoring the consequences of bad choices.

If you are in financial trouble, you must determine to pay off your debts. It will require great discipline and perhaps some pain, but this is not a time to feel sorry for yourself. Taking responsibility to solve the problem is for you to do.

It takes time to get into debt, and it takes time to get out of debt. Cooperate with God in dealing with it.

GOD'S WORD FOR YOU

Do you not know that your body is the temple (the very sanctuary) of the Holy Spirit Who lives within you, Whom you have received [as a Gift] from God? You are not your own . . .

1 CORINTHIANS 6:19

BALANCE IN YOUR DIET

If I don't determine to stick to a sensible diet, I will find something I like and eat it all the time. Of course, that is not wise because the human body was never meant to live off of sweets and snacks. We cannot eat only ice cream, candy bars, and potato chips and expect to stay healthy.

There is nothing worse than going through life feeling bad all the time. As a person who struggled for years with eating and weight problems, I know the feeling all too well. When we eat the wrong foods and put on extra pounds, we just don't feel right.

God calls each of us to do something special in this life. But to do it, we must determine to take care of our body—the house we live in. We have to find balance in what we eat and drink, get enough rest and exercise, and keep our weight down to what is right for our frame.

I don't think that anyone will be healthy without following a balanced diet. Each of us needs to know our body, what it needs, and what is really best for it. Determine today that you will begin to eat better and live free.

You are free to follow the leading of the Holy Spirit and free from doing everything your flesh demands.

For God did not give us a spirit of timidity (of cowardice, of craven and cringing and fawning fear), but [He has given us a spirit] of power and of love and of calm and well-balanced mind and discipline and self-control.

2 TIMOTHY 1:7

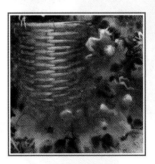

Balance in Everything

It's possible to go overboard in any area of our life. A woman can ruin her marriage by getting excessively involved in spiritual activities, such as praying and Bible studies. If she fails to pay attention to her husband's needs, no amount of spiritual reasons will compensate for the damage to her relationship.

Men have a great need for recreation and want to have fun. For some men, that need is turned into an obsession that consumes them.

Some people don't think enough, while others think too much. Some don't talk enough, and some talk too much. Some people plan too much, and some don't plan enough. Sometimes we think too highly of ourselves, and sometimes we think too lowly of ourselves. We can spend too much time on ourselves, becoming selfish and self-centered. But we can also ignore ourselves and our own needs so much that it causes deep emotional problems. Sometimes we all need to do just a little something for ourselves.

God is merciful and works with us to bring order to our lives. Take whatever steps and make whatever adjustments He is showing you.

GOD'S WORD FOR YOU

Moses' father-in-law said to him, The thing that you are doing is not good.

You will surely wear out both yourself and this people with you, for the thing is too heavy for you; you are not able to perform it all by yourself.

EXODUS 18:17–18

You Are Not Invincible

It would not surprise me to learn that God is saying the same thing to you that He said to Moses. It is a word for today. Sometimes we like to think we are invincible. We don't like anybody to tell us that something is too much for us to handle, and we push on and on despite what we feel.

I was always the kind of person who thought I could do anything I set my mind to. I was thoroughly convinced I could do all things through Christ Who strengthens me. If someone told me differently, it just made me more determined. I found out that if we have an attitude that we can do anything, no matter what it is, we are out of balance. It took some health problems to prove it to me.

Here's the truth: God does not give us power for anything He does not tell us to do. God does not give us more than we can stand or endure. If He gives us a job to do, then He gives us the ability to perform it. And I don't mean just dragging ourselves around half dead all the time. God means for you to have life and to have it abundantly.

Are there any adjustments you need to make in order to keep yourself in balance? If you will adjust, as Moses did, you will slam the door in the devil's face.

But he himself went a day's journey into the wilderness and came and sat down under a lone broom or juniper tree and asked that he might die. He said, It is enough; now, O Lord, take away my life; for I am no better than my fathers.

As he lay asleep under the broom or juniper tree, behold, an angel touched him and said to him, Arise and eat.

He looked, and behold, there was a cake baked on the coals, and a bottle of water at his head. And he ate and drank and lay down again.

The angel of the Lord came the second time and touched him and said, Arise and eat, for the journey is too great for you.

So he arose and ate and drank, and went in the strength of that food forty days and nights to Horeb, the mount of God.

1 KINGS 19:4–8

*G*ET SOME REST

Why in the world would a man such as Elijah, who on the previous day had triumphed over 450 prophets of Baal, suddenly allow himself to become so intimidated by the threats of a solitary woman named Jezebel that he ran away in fear?

If you study the story closely, it's clear that he was totally worn out and exhausted from pushing himself so hard for so long. Even an extraordinary anointing of the Spirit does not mean you won't get tired. Elijah's body was completely broken down, and his emotions had totally fallen apart. He was not handling himself the way he normally would. He was afraid, depressed, discouraged, and suicidal.

Nothing in life looks good to us when we are exhausted. It seems to us that nobody loves us, nobody helps us, nobody is concerned about us. We feel abused, misused, misunderstood, and mistreated. Many times when we feel we have deep problems, all that is wrong with us is that we are exhausted.

The Lord said to Elijah, "You're worn out. You need a couple of hot meals and a good night's rest." We need to listen to that word.

Many of the problems people have in relationships today are the result of imbalance—just being worn out.

GOD'S WORD FOR YOU

I am the True Vine, and My Father is the Vinedresser. Any branch in Me that does not bear fruit [that stops bearing] He cuts away (trims off, takes away); and He cleanses and repeatedly prunes every branch that continues to bear fruit, to make it bear more and richer and more excellent fruit. . . .

When you bear (produce) much fruit, My Father is honored and glorified, and you show and prove yourselves to be true followers of Mine.

JOHN 15:1–2, 8

DETERMINE TO PRUNE

Lack of balance hinders fruitful living. And if there is anything that God wants us to do, it is to bear fruit. The first thing God said to Adam and Eve was, "Be fruitful." Jesus made it clear in John 15 that He desires us to be fruit-bearing disciples.

Jesus says that if we do not bear fruit, God will prune us to make us productive. And if we do bear fruit, God will prune us so we bear more, richer, and more excellent fruit. To us the word *prune* is a nasty, ugly word because it means to "cut away," "trim off," or "take away." Nobody likes those cutting words. But it's clear that we are going to be pruned.

God may have to clip off some things in our lives that we would like to baby and nurse along. It may mean letting go of things we're doing that we're very comfortable with. It may mean significant change to adjust to. But God knows what He has in mind for us overall. When He starts dealing with us to let go of something, the best thing we can do is just let it go because He knows His business.

When we are determined to give up our way of doing things and accept God's way of doing things, we are on the road to becoming all that God wants us to be.

I WILL
PRESS ON

God is on your side, and if He is for you, it really does not matter who is against you. The giants may be big, but God is bigger. You may have weaknesses, but God has strength. You may have sin in your life, but God has grace. You may fail, but God remains faithful!

GOD'S WORD FOR YOU

Now to Him Who, by (in consequence of) the [action of His] power that is at work within us, is able to [carry out His purpose and] do superabundantly, far over and above all that we [dare] ask or think [infinitely beyond our highest prayers, desires, thoughts, hopes, or dreams] . . .

EPHESIANS 3:20

six

I WILL PRESS ON

od loves to use common, ordinary, everyday people who have uncommon goals and visions.

That is what I am—just a common, ordinary person with a goal and vision that fuel my determination. But just because I am common and ordinary does not mean that I am content to be average. I don't like that word. I don't want to be average. I don't intend to be average. I don't serve an average God; therefore, I don't believe I have to be average—and neither do you.

I believe that anyone can be mightily used by God. I believe that we can do great and mighty things, things that amaze even us, if we believe that God can use us and if we will be daring and determined enough to have an uncommon goal and vision. By uncommon I mean something that we truly have to believe God for— beyond all that we could dare to hope, ask, or think, according to His great power that is at work in us. We need to be daring in our faith and in our prayers.

We must determine to stretch our faith into new realms. We need to be common people with uncommon goals.

GOD'S WORD FOR YOU

For [simply] consider your own call, brethren; not many
[of you were considered to be] wise according to human
estimates and standards, not many influential and powerful,
not many of high and noble birth.

[No] for God selected (deliberately chose) what in the
world is foolish to put the wise to shame, and what the world
calls weak to put the strong to shame.

And God also selected (deliberately chose) what in the
world is lowborn and insignificant and branded and treated
with contempt, even the things that are nothing, that He
might depose and bring to nothing the things that are,

So that no mortal man should [have pretense for
glorying and] boast in the presence of God.

1 CORINTHIANS 1:26–29

CHOSEN BY GOD

Paul tells us plainly what God chooses and why. He says that He chooses what to the world is foolish to put the wise to shame, and what the world calls weak to put the strong to shame.

I am so glad it tells me that God deliberately chose me. He didn't get me by accident. I wasn't just pushed off on Him so that He had no choice but to carry on this ministry through me because He couldn't get anyone else to do it.

When God got the idea for Life In The Word Ministries, He looked around for the biggest mess He could find, someone who loved Him and had a right heart toward Him, someone who would work hard, someone who was determined, diligent, and disciplined. But I had no special talent. The only thing I do really well is talk, but even my voice is a bit unusual.

People look at the exterior, but God looks at the heart. His choice is not based on appearance, education, our possessions, or even our talents. It is based on our heart attitude, whether we are willing to fulfill a handful of qualifications to be used by God.

If we continue being faithful to God, we will eventually get where God wants us to be.

GOD'S WORD FOR YOU

I appeal to you therefore, brethren, and beg of you in view of [all] the mercies of God, to make a decisive dedication of your bodies [presenting all your members and faculties] as a living sacrifice, holy (devoted, consecrated) and well pleasing to God, which is your reasonable (rational, intelligent) service and spiritual worship.

ROMANS 12:1

$\mathscr{B}$E USABLE

If you are a believer, your life has been consecrated to God, set apart for His use only. You don't belong to yourself, because you have been bought with a price (1 Corinthians 6:20). You have the brand of the Holy Spirit upon you (Ephesians 4:30), just as a rancher brands his cattle to show that they belong to him.

We should not have the attitude that God belongs to us and try to tell Him what we want and how He should go about getting it for us. We should not start every morning by giving God our twelve-part want list of what it is going to take to make us happy. But I spent years doing that. I used to pray, "Oh, God, if I don't have more money, I just can't stand it." Those were the wilderness years for my life.

Our problem is that too often we think about what we cannot do rather than what we can do. Whatever God requires of us, we can do. What He requires of us is simply to be usable, and all of us can do that. We can work hard, walk in wisdom, and try to make sure that our words and thoughts are pleasing to God while we trust Him to work out His good plan for our life.

We may not be able to do everything, but we can finish what God gives us to start. We can stay on the narrow path. We can be committed and disciplined.

GOD'S WORD FOR YOU

For I know the thoughts and plans that I have for you,
says the Lord, thoughts and plans for welfare and peace
and not for evil, to give you hope in your final outcome.

JEREMIAH 29:11

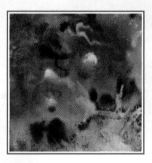

God Has a Plan

The most important thing is not how we start but how we finish. Some people get started with a bang, but they never finish. Others are slow starters, but they finish strong.

God has a plan for each of us. It is our destiny. But it is a possibility, not a "positively." Even if someone prophesies over us wonderful things in the name of the Lord, just as a prophet did with me, what is being prophesied is the heart, the will, and the desire of God for us. It doesn't mean it is positively going to happen, because if we don't cooperate with God, it is not going to come to pass. We have a part to play in seeing that plan come true. God cannot do anything in our lives without our cooperation.

I challenge you to cooperate with God every single day of your life to develop your potential. Every day you should learn something new. Every day you should grow. Every day you should be a bit further along than you were the day before.

We must each discover our own God-given gifts and talents, what we are truly capable of, and then put ourselves to the task of developing those gifts, talents, and capabilities to their fullest extent.

GOD'S WORD FOR YOU

Do not be conformed to this world (this age), [fashioned after and adapted to its external, superficial customs], but be transformed (changed) by the [entire] renewal of your mind [by its new ideals and its new attitude], so that you may prove [for yourselves] what is the good and acceptable and perfect will of God, even the thing which is good and acceptable and perfect [in His sight for you].

ROMANS 12:2

Go Against the Flow

John Mason wrote two very good books that I recommend you read. One is entitled *An Enemy Called Average*, and the other is titled *Conquering an Enemy Called Average*. One expression of his that I really like is this: "Know your limits, then ignore them." That's what I do. I know what I can't do and what I can do. I have decided to concentrate on what I can do, not what I can't do.

Too many people concentrate on everything they do wrong and never on what they do right. They get so caught up in their mistakes that they lose sight of the fact that we serve a great God. Sometimes our own inabilities distract us from looking to Jesus.

Mason also says, "The most unprofitable item ever manufactured is an excuse." People make up excuses for why they don't do anything. "I can't. It's too hard." Mother Teresa went to India with three pennies and God, and she didn't do badly.

Take an inventory. What are you doing with your time, energy, talents, abilities, and life? Are you just following everybody else? Go against the flow!

*If you can only do one thing, make up your mind
that you are going to do that one thing well.
Be the best at that one thing you can do.*

GOD'S WORD FOR YOU

Therefore He says, Awake, O sleeper, and arise from the dead, and Christ shall shine (make day dawn) upon you and give you light.

Look carefully then how you walk! Live purposefully and worthily and accurately, not as the unwise and witless, but as wise (sensible, intelligent people),

Making the very most of the time [buying up each opportunity], because the days are evil.

Therefore do not be vague and thoughtless and foolish, but understanding and firmly grasping what the will of the Lord is.

EPHESIANS 5:14–17

KNOW WHAT YOU'RE DOING

Do you know what the will of God is for you? Do you have a vision that fuels the power of your determination? Do you know what you are going to do with your life? You should.

Now obviously, if you're just starting out on the Christian walk, you may not know your future. But God will give you something to start doing, and it will become clearer as you obey each step. But if you are forty or fifty years old, you should know God's will for your life.

I got ahold of this passage in Ephesians many years ago when God first called me into the ministry. In those days I was such a mess that I would sit on my couch after I had put the kids down for a nap and cry for two hours. That is all I knew to do back then. I was mad at Dave, had a chip on my shoulder, and had many other problems as well. Yet I was teaching a home Bible study and I loved God, and it was the will of God. It was my starting spot.

Paul tells us that we should not be vague about God's will, but we should understand and firmly grasp it.

We need to be people of purpose. We need to know why we are doing what we are doing and not lose sight of our goal.

GOD'S WORD FOR YOU

Also [Jesus] told them a parable to the effect that they ought always to pray and not to turn coward (faint, lose heart, and give up).

LUKE 18:1

REFUSE TO GIVE UP

It is easy to drift backward, but we must press forward. Effortless living is never effective. Everyone thinks that the more we can get ahold of with no effort, the better life is, but that is a lie.

One thing that is wrong with us Americans today, even with our health, is the fact that we don't have much of anything to do but go through life pushing buttons—the elevator, the dishwasher, the washing machine. Just push a button and away we go. Still we gripe and grumble because we have to load and unload the machines!

We were not created to have an effortless life. We were created for work, involvement, participation, and struggle. We are not supposed to struggle with everything, but we are also not supposed to be the kind of people who quit and give up easily.

There are numerous examples of people in the Bible who simply refused to give up. Zacchaeus could not be kept from Jesus, despite his shortcomings. The woman with the issue of blood pressed through the crowd and was rewarded for her determination. This is how we reach our objectives.

The apostle Paul said that the most important thing he did was to forget what lies behind and press on.

GOD'S WORD FOR YOU

In the fourth year of Jehoiakim son of Josiah king of
Judah, this word came to Jeremiah from the Lord:

Take a scroll [of parchment] for a book and write on it
all the words I have spoken to you against Israel and Judah
and all the nations from the day I spoke to you in the days
of [King] Josiah until this day.

JEREMIAH 36:1–2

DO IT AGAIN!

When Jeremiah wrote this scroll, he was actually under house arrest. Certain people could visit him, but he couldn't go out. He was still receiving prophecies from the Lord and writing them down. Then one of his servants would come and carry the message throughout the land. God is not put off by inconveniences; He always finds another way to get His work done.

God gave Jeremiah a prophecy about Israel and Judah and ordered him to record it. Writing in the days of quill and ink on a scroll was a tedious job, and if copies were needed, it was long and painstaking. When the king heard about the scroll and had it brought to the royal palace and read to him, he didn't like what it said. The king enjoyed his unrighteous lifestyle, and he didn't want to change. So he cut up and burned the scroll page after page until it was all gone.

After all that, what was God's response? "Jeremiah, go get yourself another scroll and write the thing over" (see Jeremiah 36:27–28). In other words, do it again.

Until we get a breakthrough and finish what God has called us to do, we need to be willing to do it again and again and again.

GOD'S WORD FOR YOU

Enter through the narrow gate; for wide is the gate and spacious and broad is the way that leads away to destruction, and many are those who are entering through it.

But the gate is narrow (contracted by pressure) and the way is straitened and compressed that leads away to life, and few are those who find it.

MATTHEW 7:13–14

$\mathscr{S}$TAY ON THE NARROW PATH

Jesus made it clear that it is easy to succumb to temptation, to fall into sin, and be destroyed. It is easy to get into the flow of the world and just float along in the worldly boat with everybody else. The world is full of compromisers today, people who are willing to make any concession and live the status quo, be average, and just get by in life.

You who have gone through the narrow gate are going to have to stand against pressure. If you are determined to talk right, act right, think right, put your money in the right place, and to stop living a selfish life, Satan is not going to make it easy for you. He hates it when we decide to be radical for God.

We resist the devil by submitting to God and staying on the narrow path. Satan may tell you that you are the only one who is going through trials and tribulations and it's all worthless. The truth is, I don't know too many people who are not going through something.

Keep in mind where the narrow path leads, and you'll never give in.

Sometimes the only people you are going to find on the narrow path are you and the Lord. If that's so, just keep going!

JOYCE MEYER

Joyce Meyer has been teaching the Word of God
since 1976 and in full-time ministry since 1980. She
is the bestselling author of over 54 inspirational
books, including *Secrets to Exceptional Living*, *The Joy
of Believing Prayer*, and *Battlefield of the Mind*, as well
as over 240 audiocassette albums and over 90 videos.
Joyce's *Life In The Word* radio and television
programs are broadcast around the world, and she
travels extensively conducting "Life In The Word"
conferences. Joyce and her husband, Dave, are
the parents of four grown children and make
their home in St. Louis, Missouri.

Additional copies of this book are available from your local bookstore.

If this book has changed your life, we would like to hear from you.

Please write us at:

Joyce Meyer Ministries
P.O. Box 655 • Fenton, MO 63026

or call: (636) 349-0303

Internet Address: www.joycemeyer.org

In Canada, write: Joyce Meyer Ministries Canada, Inc.
Lambeth Box 1300 • London, ON N6P 1T5

or call: (636) 349-0303

In Australia, write: Joyce Meyer Ministries—Australia
Locked Bag 77 • Mansfield Delivery Centre
Queensland 4122

or call: (07) 3349 1200

In England, write: Joyce Meyer Ministries
P.O. Box 1549 • Windsor • SL4 1GT

or call: 01753 831102